Manda Education™

Verbal Boot Camp for the SSAT® Upper

365 Questions on Synonyms and Analogies

Verbal Boot Camp for the SSAT® Upper

365 Questions on Synonyms and Analogies

Editorial:
Justin Grosslight, head author

eBook ISBN: 978-0-9974232-4-2

Note that SSAT is a registered trademark of the Secondary School Admission Test Board, which neither sponsors nor endorses this product.

TABLE OF CONTENTS:

WHAT IS THE PURPOSE OF THIS BOOK?

Preparing for the verbal section of the SSAT can be a challenging task for many students, particularly if their vocabulary repertoire is limited (this is especially true for international students whose first language is not English). The English language contains tens of thousands of words, and guessing which ones will appear on the SSAT can be a tough task. This book is intended to provide you with exposure to several hundred words that have frequently appeared on exams for high school admissions and college admissions tests. Practicing the questions contained in this text is a good means of learning new and exciting words.

At the same time, we realize that practicing questions should be just part of a regimen to improve one's vocabulary. Often students begin preparing for the SSAT verbal exam too late and are forced to cram long lists of words in a short time – only to forget many of the words after the exam is over. Complementing practice questions with sustained, active reading of intellectual and/or academic materials (not from school textbooks) is the best way to improve one's vocabulary. These habits, combined with regular review of vocabulary – flash cards can be a good idea – often produce the best results. As for this book, it is intended for anyone seeking a verbal workout challenge, especially for students in grades 8 through 10 who plan to take the SSAT upper exam.

A note to consider: many of the words on the SSAT verbal exam are very difficult and are well above an early high school vocabulary level. Parents should not panic about performances in this book or on test day itself that seem out of step with their child's abilities. Though SSAT scores are important, the application process to private American boarding schools is holistic and considers grades, interviews, essays, recommendations, extracurricular activities, and other factors as part of the admissions process. Nonetheless, with proper practice, guidance and encouragement, anybody can improve his or her chances of SSAT success.

SYNONYMS

Each of the following questions consists of one word followed by five words or phrases. You are to select the one word or phrase whose meaning is closest to the word in capital letters.

1. PERIL

(A) danger
(B) entertainment
(C) type of jewelry
(D) childlike
(E) entertaining

2. SCEPTER

(A) hat
(B) robe
(C) staff
(D) sewage
(E) crown

3. FERVENT

(A) creative
(B) outdated
(C) bored
(D) tiring
(E) passionate

4. DEBACLE

(A) endeavor
(B) success
(C) disaster
(D) fight
(E) quandary

5. OMINOUS

(A) passion
(B) dearth
(C) pleasant
(D) foreboding
(E) thriving

6. INANE

(A) funny
(B) curious
(C) silly
(D) charming
(E) strange

7. CONNOISSEUR

(A) novice
(B) expert
(C) politician
(D) overlord
(E) chef

8. DYNAMIC

(A) explosive
(B) charming
(C) stagnant
(D) persuasive
(E) energetic

9. MAR

(A) appease
(B) concern
(C) damage
(D) clarify
(E) garble

4

10.   SACCHARINE

(A)   very bitter
(B)   too sweet
(C)   bland
(D)   salty
(E)   appetizing

11.   QUIVER

(A)   smile
(B)   grimace
(C)   tremble
(D)   panic
(E)   eat

12.   BUOYANT

(A)   cheerful
(B)   gloomy
(C)   thrilled
(D)   disinterested
(E)   charming

13.   REVERENT

(A)   concerned
(B)   respectful
(C)   unusual
(D)   terrific
(E)   inverted

14.   OMIT

(A)   exaggerate
(B)   portend
(C)   bungle
(D)   fleece
(E)   leave out

15. PALLID

(A) pale
(B) burning
(C) knightly
(D) spirited
(E) clever

16. CALLOUS

(A) obedient
(B) cute
(C) kind
(D) insensitive
(E) embarrassed

17. CRUX

(A) crossroads
(B) key idea
(C) chicken bone
(D) assistance
(E) armor

18. BAR

(A) protect
(B) admit
(C) block
(D) expunge
(E) exhaust

19. FLAG

(A) lack energy
(B) seek promise
(C) be judgmental
(D) be hungry
(E) feel rejected

20.   LANGUISH

(A)   lacking vitality
(B)   showing glee
(C)   feeling envy
(D)   having curiosity
(E)   feeling ill

21.   BROOK

(A)   bridge
(B)   rock
(C)   small stream
(D)   waterfall
(E)   pond

22.   ZEAL

(A)   inquisitiveness
(B)   resentment
(C)   lassitude
(D)   ardor
(E)   happiness

23.   FORTIFY

(A)   strengthen
(B)   weaken
(C)   defend
(D)   illuminate
(E)   alloy

24.   ACCOLADE

(A)   worry
(B)   praise
(C)   fear
(D)   legitimacy
(E)   beverage

25.   BEDLAM

(A)   stability
(B)   complexity
(C)   chaos
(D)   intrigue
(E)   normalcy

26.   PEDESTRIAN

(A)   atypical
(B)   unique
(C)   ordinary
(D)   uncouth
(E)   ironic

27.   LAX

(A)   not strict
(B)   tired
(C)   recreational
(D)   strict
(E)   hungry

28.   EDIBLE

(A)   can be eaten
(B)   drinkable
(C)   odorous
(D)   empty
(E)   pleasing

29.   NADIR

(A)   flat
(B)   rugged
(C)   zenith
(D)   environmental
(E)   lowest point

30. VEX

(A) appease
(B) befuddle
(C) elaborate
(D) annoy
(E) harm

31. GARRULOUS

(A) annoying
(B) loquacious
(C) timorous
(D) extended
(E) bungled

32. DESPONDENT

(A) soulful
(B) careful
(C) suspicious
(D) irrelevant
(E) hopeless

33. TERMINATE

(A) commence
(B) expand
(C) end
(D) regulate
(E) deflate

34. LIMBER

(A) rigid
(B) rubbery
(C) sinewy
(D) supple
(E) ample

35. CREDIBLE

(A) confused
(B) believable
(C) gracious
(D) humorous
(E) jolly

36. DEPLORE

(A) detest
(B) enamor
(C) heal
(D) query
(E) instill

37. INCUMBENT

(A) someone already in office
(B) aspirant for office
(C) officer
(D) policeman
(E) sniper

38. OBESE

(A) corpulent
(B) gaunt
(C) evolved
(D) chubby
(E) angular

39. EGRESS

(A) flight
(B) style
(C) exit
(D) entry
(E) timeless

40. BELLIGERENT

(A) affable
(B) enthusiastic
(C) smitten
(D) charming
(E) cantankerous

41. CORRIDOR

(A) type of clothing
(B) musical style
(C) long hallway
(D) artistic talent
(E) committed person

42. ITINERANT

(A) layered
(B) structured
(C) stationary
(D) intrinsic
(E) nomadic

43. VOGUE

(A) outdated
(B) questionable
(C) smart
(D) fashionable
(E) murky

44. EXTRANEOUS

(A) too much
(B) irrelevant
(C) fundamental
(D) comical
(E) protracted

45. RUPTURE

(A) stitch
(B) burst
(C) scar
(D) flow
(E) scythe

46. RELINQUISH

(A) amend
(B) extend
(C) give up
(D) fix
(E) win

47. BUCOLIC

(A) urban
(B) populated
(C) rustic
(D) complementary
(E) aged

48. ONUS

(A) extra payment
(B) burden
(C) suspicion
(D) sign of something to come
(E) clarity

49. CONVENTIONAL

(A) heterodox
(B) confusing
(C) contemporary
(D) timely
(E) orthodox

12

50. HETEROGENEOUS

(A) uniform
(B) filtered
(C) successful
(D) sorted
(E) diverse

51. YEARN

(A) sate
(B) crave
(C) explode
(D) crumble
(E) reduce

52. TORPID

(A) invigorated
(B) lethargic
(C) confounded
(D) discombobulated
(E) horrendous

53. PLAUSIBLE

(A) incredible
(B) incredulous
(C) creative
(D) believable
(E) healthy

54. ELUCIDATE

(A) confuse
(B) clarify
(C) drive
(D) complain
(E) arrange

55. QUARANTINE

(A) enamor
(B) belittle
(C) isolate
(D) discard
(E) evoke

56. SQUANDER

(A) rearrange
(B) waste
(C) salvage
(D) disparage
(E) bemoan

57. PILFER

(A) clean
(B) steal
(C) warn
(D) scold
(E) implant

58. ELOQUENT

(A) smooth
(B) coarse
(C) persuasive speaking
(D) disorganized
(E) fallacious

59. QUELL

(A) type of bird
(B) suppress
(C) expand
(D) write out
(E) lengthen

14

60.   ANACHRONISTIC

(A)   outdated
(B)   disoriented
(C)   chronological
(D)   scattered
(E)   belonging to wrong time period

61.   INGENUITY

(A)   inexperience
(B)   cleverness
(C)   attractiveness
(D)   friendliness
(E)   usefulness

62.   FLIPPANT

(A)   disrespectful
(B)   excitable
(C)   wavering
(D)   supportive
(E)   mercurial

63.   BENEVOLENCE

(A)   toleration
(B)   empathy
(C)   kindness
(D)   loyalty
(E)   utility

64.   TREPIDATION

(A)   secretive
(B)   anger
(C)   thrill
(D)   apathy
(E)   fear

65. ANOMALY

(A) aberration
(B) consistency
(C) silent
(D) soiled
(E) spoiled

66. WAX

(A) ebb
(B) grow
(C) wane
(D) liquidate
(E) enmesh

67. FRUGAL

(A) fruity
(B) expensive
(C) thrifty
(D) discounted
(E) alarming

68. STYMIE

(A) pavement
(B) flowery
(C) thwart
(D) elaborate
(E) splice

69. TRUNCATE

(A) store
(B) adjust
(C) dominate
(D) cut off
(E) add

16

70. MAGNANIMITY

(A) omniscience
(B) silence
(C) profundity
(D) control
(E) generosity

71. JEER

(A) to laugh at
(B) to scoff at
(C) to praise
(D) to loathe
(E) to admire

72. SATIRE

(A) car part
(B) planet
(C) poem
(D) parody
(E) parade

73. GLIB

(A) insincere
(B) lighthearted
(C) perplexing
(D) forensic
(E) sticky

74. HOVEL

(A) appliance for removing snow
(B) cheap hotel
(C) squalid dwelling
(D) political office
(E) oversized bathroom

75. PARADOX

(A) contradictory but true
(B) inverted
(C) ruse
(D) two of something
(E) a beautiful place

76. REGAL

(A) majestic bird
(B) royal
(C) obsequious
(D) decorous
(E) idiosyncratic

77. CONNIVING

(A) scheming
(B) salivating
(C) rousing
(D) admiring
(E) bereaving

78. OLFACTORY

(A) concerning taste
(B) concerning sight
(C) concerning smell
(D) concerning hearing
(E) concerning touch

79. NOSTALGIA

(A) expecting
(B) longing for the past
(C) awaiting the future
(D) imagining
(E) loathing

18

80.   BANE

(A)   charm
(B)   incense
(C)   source of harm
(D)   amusing show
(E)   hurt

81.   PUNGENT

(A)   strong smelling
(B)   discolored
(C)   dangerous
(D)   wet
(E)   oily

82.   OBSOLETE

(A)   timely
(B)   luminous
(C)   hibernating
(D)   outmoded
(E)   misshaped

83.   LUCRATIVE

(A)   broke
(B)   tax free
(C)   very profitable
(D)   miserly
(E)   altruistic

84.   TRENCHANT

(A)   unclear
(B)   cogent
(C)   mellifluous
(D)   organized
(E)   incisive

85. COMMEMORATION

(A) souvenir
(B) memorial celebration
(C) birthday party
(D) memento
(E) anniversary

86. DOGMA

(A) set of principles
(B) canine quality
(C) spiritual philosophy
(D) authoritarian
(E) obsequious

87. THRIVE

(A) writhe
(B) sonorous
(C) flourish
(D) quash
(E) stifle

88. ENIGMATIC

(A) entertaining
(B) insensitive
(C) spoiled
(D) cryptic
(E) furtive

89. WARY

(A) hostile
(B) suspicious
(C) demanding
(D) trusting
(E) earnest

20

90.   LAMBASTE

(A)   baste
(B)   roast
(C)   bathe
(D)   broil
(E)   criticize harshly

91.   NEFARIOUS

(A)   filial
(B)   wicked
(C)   concerned
(D)   fearless
(E)   domineering

92.   QUENCH

(A)   satisfy
(B)   relieve
(C)   complicate
(D)   bemuse
(E)   mince

93.   CASTIGATE

(A)   behead
(B)   heal a wound
(C)   scold
(D)   censor
(E)   omit

94.   INTREPID

(A)   inspiring
(B)   fearless
(C)   terrifying
(D)   terrible
(E)   native

95. PERJURE

(A) to lie in court
(B) to testify
(C) to sharpen
(D) to cast a spell
(E) to stir up

96. KINETIC

(A) static
(B) imaginative
(C) torrid
(D) gliding
(E) dynamic

97. MEEK

(A) happy
(B) daunting
(C) foreboding
(D) timid
(E) practical

98. GREGARIOUS

(A) pleasant
(B) sociable
(C) solitary
(D) quixotic
(E) amenable

99. IMPAIR

(A) damage
(B) spur
(C) classify
(D) archive
(E) reorder

100. MISCREANT

(A) poorly constructed
(B) law-breaking person
(C) vile habit
(D) deformed creature
(E) handicapped entry

101. KNELL

(A) solemn ring
(B) soup dumpling
(C) buzzing sound
(D) gold nugget
(E) storage space

102. BENEFICIAL

(A) disoriented
(B) useful
(C) myopic
(D) holy
(E) lachrymose

103. DENIGRATE

(A) inspire
(B) enervate
(C) belittle
(D) deny
(E) brag

104. SORDID

(A) comely
(B) organized
(C) petty
(D) humble
(E) base

105. PLETHORA

(A) dearth
(B) excess
(C) need
(D) loss
(E) average

106. NOISOME

(A) quiet
(B) silent
(C) malodorous
(D) aromatic
(E) loud

107. BLATANT

(A) subtle
(B) variegated
(C) striped
(D) pied
(E) obvious

108. INCLEMENT

(A) inclined
(B) tilted
(C) bad weather
(D) step by step
(E) durable

109. EPHEMERAL

(A) timeless
(B) temporary
(C) permanent
(D) sporadic
(E) random

110. HERMIT

(A) misanthrope
(B) person in solitude
(C) stranger
(D) outlaw
(E) thief

111. FIASCO

(A) music genre
(B) pet food
(C) debacle
(D) success
(E) annual event

112. STELLAR

(A) pitiful
(B) confounding
(C) manipulative
(D) insensible
(E) amazing

113. HUSBANDRY

(A) concerning divorce
(B) concerning marriage
(C) concerning cultivating crops and animals
(D) concerning one's family relations
(E) concerning time

114. PRETEXT

(A) preface
(B) introduction
(C) subtitle
(D) excuse
(E) defense

115. MAUDLIN

(A) acerbic
(B) overly sentimental
(C) plaintive
(D) riveting
(E) cozy

116. NEPOTISM

(A) favoring family
(B) loving friends
(C) winning games
(D) spending time with nephews
(E) praising new things

117. PROSAIC

(A) type of medicine
(B) captivating
(C) dull text
(D) collage
(E) long memo

118. EXONERATE

(A) free from blame
(B) escape
(C) destroy
(D) cut out
(E) shorten

119. SURMISE

(A) suppose
(B) savor
(C) lavish
(D) fear
(E) create

120. EMIT

(A) produce and discharge
(B) leave out
(C) cancel
(D) focus
(E) swarm

121. INERT

(A) energized
(B) incapable
(C) motionless
(D) flexible
(E) oscillating

122. WINCE

(A) grimace in distress
(B) smile in excitement
(C) yell in anger
(D) cough in disagreement
(E) laugh in embarrassment

123. ACRIMONY

(A) bitterness
(B) gleefulness
(C) aptitude
(D) inclination
(E) disaster

124. NEOPHYTE

(A) expert
(B) veteran
(C) referee
(D) tyro
(E) mineral

125. LUMBER

(A) wood cabin
(B) move slowly and awkwardly
(C) move gracefully
(D) bend rapidly
(E) paint thoroughly

126. POSITIVE

(A) depressing
(B) convoluted
(C) rising
(D) optimistic
(E) emotional

127. COERCION

(A) forced persuasion
(B) charm
(C) flattery
(D) advertise
(E) suspend

128. UTOPIA

(A) metropolis
(B) archipelago
(C) ideal place
(D) catastrophe
(E) giant let down

129. FLAMBOYANT

(A) fiery
(B) incompetent
(C) reflective
(D) youthful
(E) showy

130. ENGROSSING

(A) make ugly
(B) confusing
(C) captivating
(D) detrimental
(E) disgusting

131. ARCANE

(A) excited
(B) esoteric
(C) philosophical
(D) magical
(E) handicapped

132. NOXIOUS

(A) discourteous
(B) beautiful
(C) elaborate
(D) harmful
(E) contemporary

133. VORACIOUS

(A) thirsty
(B) starving
(C) ravenous
(D) vegetarian
(E) satiated

134. MELANCHOLY

(A) agitated
(B) sad
(C) amicable
(D) emotionless
(E) worrisome

135. INSOMNIA

(A) sleepwalking
(B) sleeplessness
(C) sleepiness
(D) too much sleep
(E) sleeping at work

136. JUBILANT

(A) type of dessert
(B) anniversary
(C) funny
(D) joyful
(E) envious

137. DOMINATE

(A) suspend
(B) intensify
(C) reorganize
(D) fall over
(E) overpower

138. PIOUS

(A) sanctimonious
(B) committed
(C) religiously devoted
(D) steadfast
(E) enamored

139. OBTUSE

(A) fat
(B) slow to understand
(C) wide
(D) clear
(E) fostered

140. SUAVE

(A) charming
(B) extensive
(C) cleanly
(D) shiny
(E) delicious

141. BANAL

(A) legible
(B) exotic
(C) dismissive
(D) reverent
(E) commonplace

142. REIMBURSE

(A) respect
(B) refund
(C) refill
(D) redo
(E) remember

143. CUPIDITY

(A) excessive desire
(B) ornateness
(C) arrogance
(D) lovesickness
(E) infatuation

144. VAGUE

(A) avant-garde
(B) limpid
(C) understandable
(D) dark
(E) unclear

145. HOAX

(A) dress
(B) soft drink
(C) guide
(D) deception
(E) summarize

146. PRICELESS

(A) affordable
(B) expensive
(C) invaluable
(D) worthy
(E) exquisite

147. MEDLEY

(A) field
(B) fencing
(C) yard
(D) mixture
(E) vegetable

148. ARID

(A) windy
(B) saturated
(C) chilly
(D) humid
(E) dry

149. FRANK

(A) fictitious
(B) dishonest
(C) avoidant
(D) candid
(E) reticent

150. DEBILITATED

(A) empowered
(B) weakened
(C) vilified
(D) attentive
(E) free

151. WRATH

(A) specter
(B) kindness
(C) anger
(D) holiday decoration
(E) control

152. GERMANE

(A) religiosity
(B) relevant
(C) attractiveness
(D) culpable
(E) mistaken

153. OPULENT

(A) concerning eyesight
(B) flashy
(C) clandestine
(D) wavering
(E) linked

154. RATIFY

(A) to pass a law
(B) to write a treaty
(C) to win a game
(D) to lose money
(E) to become ill

155. FASTIDIOUS

(A) rapid
(B) disheveled
(C) slow
(D) scrupulous
(E) clever

156. CALAMITY

(A) triumph
(B) disaster
(C) loud noise
(D) crash
(E) burst

157. SURFEIT

(A) ocean sport
(B) landless peasant
(C) excess
(D) paucity
(E) exclamation

158. ENDORSE

(A) deny
(B) support
(C) create
(D) solicit
(E) inquire

159. IGNITE

(A) snuff out
(B) construct
(C) spark
(D) relax
(E) evening party

160. POLEMICAL

(A) peaceful
(B) artistic
(C) conversational
(D) exciting
(E) contentious

161. BANISH

(A) clean up
(B) settle
(C) return
(D) cast out
(E) accrue

162. CONCUR

(A) demoralize
(B) agree
(C) dissolve
(D) mention
(E) refrain

163. TACTFUL

(A) blunt
(B) sharp
(C) honed
(D) coarse
(E) discreet

164. CADENCE

(A) tessellation
(B) rhythm
(C) organization
(D) emotion
(E) isolation

165. ABHOR

(A) hate
(B) thrill
(C) resent
(D) embolden
(E) dislike

166. STEALTHY

(A) ferocious
(B) artsy
(C) cute
(D) crafty
(E) humble

167. DOZE

(A) nap
(B) boast
(C) deviate
(D) twelve of something
(E) batter

168. AVARICE

(A) obsequiousness
(B) trickery
(C) equanimity
(D) greed
(E) redundancy

169. FATAL

(A) predestined
(B) deadly
(C) mortal
(D) temporary
(E) indefinite

170. MALLEABLE

(A) poor
(B) shapeable
(C) rigid
(D) oblong
(E) sharp

171. RECUR

(A) happen again
(B) surprise
(C) distress
(D) plague
(E) annoy

172. SURLY

(A) entertaining
(B) tepid
(C) twisting
(D) sloped
(E) unfriendly

173. NEBULOUS

(A) stringy
(B) webbed
(C) arrogant
(D) assured
(E) unclear

174. AILMENT

(A) alcohol
(B) illness
(C) potion
(D) cauldron
(E) barrel

175. GULLIBLE

(A) ditch
(B) credulous
(C) tenable
(D) imaginary
(E) pliable

176. FATIGUE

(A) overweight
(B) inspiration
(C) nourishment
(D) donut
(E) exhaustion

177. PRUNE

(A) dry out
(B) trim shrubs
(C) grow fruit
(D) cut plums
(E) yield

178. MORTIFY

(A) please
(B) implement
(C) simmer
(D) irritate
(E) shock

179. STRIDENT

(A) melodic
(B) blurry
(C) progressive
(D) fast paced
(E) shrill

180. FLEDGLING

(A) trained
(B) newborn
(C) inexperienced
(D) foul
(E) jammed

181. MILIEU

(A) ambiance
(B) one thousand year
(C) milky
(D) sweet
(E) carnival

182. APOCRYPHAL

(A) end of the world
(B) spurious
(C) authentic
(D) supernatural
(E) written

183. OMNIPOTENT

(A) all knowing
(B) ubiquitous
(C) weak
(D) controlling
(E) all powerful

184. EXPEDITE

(A) eject
(B) speed up
(C) forget
(D) outweigh
(E) run out

185. GOUGE

(A) measure
(B) allow
(C) scoop
(D) strain
(E) scrape

186. PALTRY

(A) pastry
(B) useful
(C) foundational
(D) insignificant
(E) necessary

187. AMBIGUOUS

(A) mixed feelings
(B) tied up
(C) exaggerated
(D) unclear
(E) mobile

188. RETICENT

(A) visual
(B) sentimental
(C) left over
(D) forgetful
(E) taciturn

189. VENERABLE

(A) revered
(B) muddled
(C) breezy
(D) disowned
(E) scrutinized

190. UNKEMPT

(A) unruly
(B) disheveled
(C) loose
(D) impolite
(E) dour

191. VEHEMENT

(A) emergency
(B) delineated
(C) passionate
(D) placid
(E) melted

192. REFUTE

(A) reject
(B) repeal
(C) redo
(D) reinstate
(E) remember

193. NAÏVE

(A) immaculate
(B) sharp
(C) well dressed
(D) innocent
(E) trained

194. MONOTONY

(A) commitment
(B) tedium
(C) energizing
(D) enervating
(E) marriage

195. CRYPTIC

(A) deadly
(B) aged
(C) mysterious
(D) inactive
(E) creepy

196. WIELD

(A) fear
(B) confuse
(C) undo
(D) generate
(E) use

197. COVET

(A) relish
(B) spurn
(C) retain
(D) copy
(E) forecast

198. OUST

(A) induce
(B) expand
(C) impel
(D) expel
(E) compel

199. GLOWER

(A) scowl
(B) fret
(C) grimace
(D) smirk
(E) smile

200. SAGE

(A) portent
(B) genius
(C) wise
(D) dreaded
(E) herbal

201. PIED

(A) full
(B) striped
(C) multicolored
(D) hungry
(E) proudness

202. DOLEFUL

(A) fruity
(B) pleasant
(C) competitive
(D) ascendant
(E) sad

203. CRESTFALLEN

(A) tragic
(B) disappointed
(C) falling
(D) broken
(E) abandoned

204. FALLOW

(A) compatriot
(B) relevant
(C) uncultivated
(D) sagging
(E) fiscal

205. URBANE

(A) metropolitan
(B) cute
(C) evil
(D) refined
(E) uneducated

206. LURID

(A) graphic
(B) seductive
(C) drastic
(D) clear
(E) rabid

207. ANODYNE

(A) refreshing
(B) inoffensive
(C) sterile
(D) peaceful
(E) entangled

208. OBDURATE

(A) rotten
(B) indolent
(C) stubborn
(D) recalcitrant
(E) moody

209. HUBRIS

(A) excessive pride
(B) empty
(C) gigantic
(D) central
(E) thriving

210. PANACEA

(A) museum
(B) cure-all
(C) all inclusive
(D) praiseful speech
(E) jail

211. APPREHENSIVE

(A) all inclusive
(B) curious
(C) thoughtful
(D) disappointing
(E) anxious

212. MIGRATE

(A) shred
(B) move about
(C) evolve
(D) change shape
(E) give birth

213. ROBUST

(A) round
(B) overweight
(C) broken
(D) vigorous
(E) robotic

214. GALACTIC

(A) concerning lighting
(B) concerning planets
(C) concerning galaxies
(D) concerning candy
(E) concerning dieting

215. REPLICATE

(A) imitate
(B) bequeath
(C) vitiate
(D) derogate
(E) redo

216. CONDONE

(A) deny
(B) test
(C) flabbergast
(D) permit
(E) mesmerize

217. DISINGENUOUS

(A) insincere
(B) disorganized
(C) unauthorized
(D) misaligned
(E) overly trusting

218. PRODIGY

(A) concerning the cosmos
(B) child genius
(C) computer program
(D) present
(E) wasteful

219. AUGMENT

(A) shock
(B) restrict
(C) horrify
(D) nudge
(E) increase

220. VAPID

(A) steamy
(B) not stimulating
(C) shiny
(D) smooth
(E) enormous

221. ENMITY

(A) nemesis
(B) competitor
(C) affectation
(D) whiner
(E) hatred

222. QUARREL

(A) type of salt
(B) sea rock
(C) resolution
(D) angry disagreement
(E) heartfelt remorse

223. JETTISON

(A) fly
(B) throw overboard
(C) hover
(D) leak
(E) promote

224. AWE

(A) sigh
(B) expression of sympathy
(C) shock
(D) speech
(E) concern

225. SARDONIC

(A) fishy
(B) disciplinary
(C) mild
(D) defensive
(E) sarcastic

226. PRECOCIOUS

(A) premature
(B) early development
(C) involving skilled negotiation
(D) predictive
(E) profound

227. MALICE

(A) peril
(B) royal home
(C) laughter
(D) ill will
(E) crystalline

228. DECORUM

(A) decorations
(B) beauty
(C) sensibility
(D) shrewdness
(E) etiquette

229. HOSTILE

(A) bitter
(B) vulgar
(C) latent
(D) jaded
(E) preachy

230. PROLIFIC

(A) successful
(B) professional
(C) positive
(D) productive
(E) simulated

231. SEVER

(A) lacerate
(B) bleed
(C) punch
(D) break off
(E) steam

232. IRE

(A) exhilaration
(B) tool for smoothing clothes
(C) serious
(D) raw mineral
(E) anger

233. CHICANERY

(A) type of factory
(B) broth
(C) trickery
(D) hospitality
(E) destruction

234. EMPIRICAL

(A) domineering
(B) majestic
(C) experimental
(D) erect
(E) imperial

235. PRISTINE

(A) pure
(B) chilled
(C) artful
(D) creative
(E) snowy

236. VINDICTIVE

(A) win
(B) prove right
(C) cruel
(D) grow
(E) corrupt

237. JUXTAPOSE

(A) vivify
(B) place side-by-side
(C) denigrate
(D) weaken
(E) bolster

238. AUSPICIOUS

(A) untrusting
(B) belittling
(C) unsettling
(D) gracious
(E) favorable

239. PANORAMA

(A) optics
(B) wide view
(C) ecumenical
(D) diversity
(E) dais

240. ENCUMBER

(A) burden
(B) fret
(C) implode
(D) depress
(E) amaze

241. QUALIFY

(A) assess
(B) access
(C) add reservations
(D) justify
(E) extrapolate

242. PRECURSOR

(A) word processor
(B) forerunner
(C) preview
(D) omen
(E) celebration

243. CHARISMA

(A) charm
(B) religiosity
(C) toxicity
(D) strain
(E) levity

244. VOLATILE

(A) serene
(B) incipient
(C) unstable
(D) trembling
(E) vicarious

245. NONCHALANT

(A) trendy
(B) emotive
(C) passive
(D) unconcerned
(E) exclamatory

ANALOGIES

The following questions ask you to find relationships between words. For each question, select the answer that best completes the meaning of the sentence.

1.   Witch is to coven as:

(A)   dog is to puppy
(B)   toddler is to adult
(C)   wolf is to pack
(D)   fish is to ocean
(E)   goose is to gander

2.   Frozen is to gelid as:

(A)   warm is to hot
(B)   wet is to dry
(C)   angry is to mellow
(D)   fury is to soothing
(E)   scorching is to blazing

3.   Saturn is to planet as:

(A)   Pacific is to Atlantic
(B)   sun is to moon
(C)   star is to asteroid
(D)   Antarctica is to continent
(E)   fjord is to inlet

4.   Parched is to inundated as:

(A)   red is to yellow
(B)   empty is to full
(C)   simple is to tragic
(D)   docile is to subjugated
(E)   juvenile is to adolescent

5.   Soporific is to sleepy as:

(A)   enticing is to relaxing
(B)   myriad is to bevy
(C)   laxative is to sedated
(D)   horrible is to gleeful
(E)   robotic is to automated

6.   Soup is to spoon as:

(A)   noodle is to knife
(B)   water is to glass
(C)   dessert is to cup
(D)   appetizer is to plate
(E)   breakfast is to chopsticks

7.   Dubious is to doubt as:

(A)   curious is to empathy
(B)   sympathy is to disorder
(C)   amusement is to indifference
(D)   thrifty is to costly
(E)   enigmatic is to confusion

8.   Sleep is to insomnia as:

(A)   food is to starvation
(B)   water is to hydration
(C)   music is to harmony
(D)   fabulous is to fantastic
(E)   gasoline is to mileage

9.   Drip is to flood as:

(A)   heavy is to massive
(B)   rotund is to elongated
(C)   furious is to enraged
(D)   spark is to conflagration
(E)   fast is to diet

10. Dalmatian is to dog as:

(A)   feline is to cat
(B)   rocky is to raccoon
(C)   macaroni is to penguin
(D)   iguana is to salamander
(E)   hare is to rabbit

11. Polish is to burnish as:

(A)   vanilla is to chocolate
(B)   delete is to erase
(C)   moist is to drenched
(D)   miffed is to livid
(E)   feather is to wing

12. Apostate is to sacrosanct as:

(A)   terrorist is to fear
(B)   cleric is to religious
(C)   outlaw is to moral
(D)   goo is to ectoplasm
(E)   bandit is to robbery

13. Architect is to electrician as:

(A)   retailer is to wholesaler
(B)   hygienist is to dentist
(C)   boss is to secretary
(D)   king is to princess
(E)   author is to printer

14. Story is to height as:

(A)   raincoat is to downpour
(B)   fathom is to depth
(C)   biography is to nonfiction
(D)   stable is to horse
(E)   insouciant is to worry

15. Roster is to names as:

(A) principal is to teacher
(B) merchandise is to warehouse
(C) parent is to child
(D) inventory is to goods
(E) buyer is to seller

16. Green is to emerald as:

(A) red is to rose
(B) white is to amethyst
(C) coal is to black
(D) pyrite is to rock
(E) blue is to sapphire

17. Pen is to writing as:

(A) tree is to chopping
(B) paper is to folding
(C) door is to locking
(D) scalpel is to surgery
(E) feet are to standing

18. Sound is to decibel as:

(A) haze is to smog
(B) inches is to snow
(C) teaspoons is to sugar
(D) distance in miles
(E) wind in knots

19. Accident is to deliberate as:

(A) trip is to stumble
(B) break is to fix
(C) harm is to heal
(D) unintentional is to devised
(E) luck is to win

20.   Comedy is to film as:

(A)   autobiography is to book
(B)   detective is to crime
(C)   soldier is to war
(D)   leader is to king
(E)   pioneer is to follower

21.   Lampoon is to mock as:

(A)   death is to cry
(B)   honor is to celebrate
(C)   love is to reject
(D)   destroy is to hope
(E)   idolize is to elevate

22.   Circle is to sphere as:

(A)   triangle is to square
(B)   round is to cylinder
(C)   rectangle is to prism
(D)   ellipse is to oval
(E)   hexagon is to polygon

23.   Baseball is to diamond as:

(A)   soccer is to team
(B)   field is to soccer
(C)   hockey is to rink
(D)   court is to basketball
(E)   goal is to soccer

24.   Kangaroo is to marsupial as:

(A)   terrier is to dog
(B)   bird is to beak
(C)   monkey is to primate
(D)   insect is to spider
(E)   horse is to stampede

25. Discordant is to sound as:

(A) soft is to touch
(B) odorous is to smell
(C) cacophony is to breeze
(D) eyesore is to sight
(E) taste is to stale

26. Sigh is to relief as:

(A) murmur is to thrill
(B) scream is to panic
(C) frown is to dissatisfaction
(D) scowl is to anger
(E) laughter is to snort

27. Caboose is to train as:

(A) cockpit is to airplane
(B) cab is to truck
(C) food court is to mall
(D) period is to sentence
(E) snooze is to oversleep

28. Cite is to acknowledge as:

(A) cancel is to ignore
(B) highlight is to emphasize
(C) abbreviate is to extend
(D) expand is to tell
(E) boil is to heat

29. Olive is to oil as:

(A) palm is to frond
(B) sugar is to candy
(C) grease is to fat
(D) cacao is to chocolate
(E) juice is to pineapple

30.   Politician is to votes as:

(A)   statistician is to data
(B)   sociologist is to people
(C)   leader is to teammates
(D)   detective is to criminal
(E)   fireman is to burn

31.   Deny is to acknowledge as:

(A)   impress is to regret
(B)   avoid is to hide
(C)   shun is to embrace
(D)   allow is to bolster
(E)   priest is to devout

32.   Nibble is to devour as:

(A)   sip is to gulp
(B)   sample is to snack
(C)   lap is to drink
(D)   taste is to try
(E)   eat is to quaff

33.   Book is to chapter as:

(A)   county is to state
(B)   land is to continent
(C)   index is to alphabetize
(D)   poem is to stanza
(E)   building is to story

34.   Toucan is to rainforest:

(A)   desert is to cactus
(B)   lion is to savanna
(C)   salmon is to aquarium
(D)   ocean is to tuna
(E)   algae is to vegetation

35.   Magnet is to attract as:

(A)   silver is to charm
(B)   thyme is to flavor
(C)   mirror is to reflect
(D)   magnifying glass is to reduce
(E)   spindle is to kill

36.   Vanquish is to suppress as:

(A)   heat is to warm
(B)   limp is to hobble
(C)   survive is to exist
(D)   mix is to stir
(E)   shatter is to crack

37.   Flourish is to decay as:

(A)   smite is to slay
(B)   restrict is to limit
(C)   thrive is to wither
(D)   languish is to excite
(E)   coalesce is to order

38.   Apprentice is to expert as:

(A)   greenhorn is to master
(B)   reader is to writer
(C)   author is to prose
(D)   pupil is to teacher
(E)   understudy is to actor

39.   Peanut is to legume as:

(A)   potato is to tomato
(B)   truffle is to fungus
(C)   cherry is to tree
(D)   okra is to cooking
(E)   apple is to cider

40.   Naysayer is to deny as:

(A)   teacher is to learn
(B)   skeptic is to doubt
(C)   policeman is to arrest
(D)   florist is to grow
(E)   physicist is to experiment

41.   Itinerary is to trip as:

(A)   agenda is to meeting
(B)   boxes are to supplies
(C)   album is to photos
(D)   toy is to store
(E)   sink is to toilet

42.   Scissors are to hair as:

(A)   bowling is to ball
(B)   car is to highway
(C)   skateboard is to ramp
(D)   bicycle is to path
(E)   lawnmower is to grass

43.   Extroverted is to outgoing as:

(A)   hasty is to emotion
(B)   cheerful is to sincere
(C)   emotional is to stable
(D)   amicable is to friendly
(E)   charming is to nonplussed

44.   Transparent is to opaque as:

(A)   milky is to clear
(B)   hurried is to rushed
(C)   open is to closed
(D)   stern is to severe
(E)   plaster is to plastic

45.   Mitigate is to assuage as:

(A)   mend is to tear
(B)   demolish is to outline
(C)   create is to abet
(D)   finish is to complete
(E)   chain is to link

46.   Emancipate is to free as:

(A)   fetter is to bind
(B)   rotate is to translate
(C)   enchant is to bewitch
(D)   entrench is to liberate
(E)   detain is to secure

47.   Cloud is to rain as:

(A)   ice is to melt
(B)   musket is to bullet
(C)   flower is to stamen
(D)   tree is to sap
(E)   bark is to dog

48.   Raze is to destroy as:

(A)   elevate is to edifice
(B)   shave is to beard
(C)   erect is to construct
(D)   fear is to tremble
(E)   curiosity is to demise

49.   Launch is to rocket as:

(A)   dribble is to ball
(B)   spring is to fall
(C)   rain is to monsoon
(D)   charge is to battery
(E)   fire is to torpedo

50.   Alibi is to abet as:

(A)   witness is to corroborate
(B)   surveyor is to measure
(C)   bystander is to forestall
(D)   judge is to believe
(E)   driver is to wait

51.   Thin is to emaciated as:

(A)   tall is to high
(B)   pudgy is to rotund
(C)   steep is to grade
(D)   cold is to hot
(E)   fuel is to combustion

52.   Tadpole is to frog as:

(A)   caterpillar is to butterfly
(B)   kid is to goat
(C)   sheep is to lamb
(D)   rooster is to hen
(E)   calf is to cow

53.   Fulcrum is to lever as:

(A)   tree house is to wood
(B)   barbell is to lift
(C)   pulley is to rope
(D)   wheel is to axle
(E)   hinge is to door

54.   Thermometer is to temperature as

(A)   plunger is to bathroom
(B)   elevator is to floor
(C)   tape is to measure
(D)   bank is to money
(E)   barometer is to pressure

55.   Baroque is to ornate as:

(A)   acerbic is to decorated
(B)   embellished is to simple
(C)   limited is to extensive
(D)   spare is to plain
(E)   intricate is to obvious

56.   Food is to famine as:

(A)   water is to drought
(B)   anxious is to terrified
(C)   heat is to temperate
(D)   ocean is to pond
(E)   try is to essay

57.   Mountain is to crater as:

(A)   cave is to dungeon
(B)   alarm is to clock
(C)   parachute is to airplane
(D)   hill is to sinkhole
(E)   basement is to attic

58.   Clarinet is to tympani as:

(A)   tuba is to horn
(B)   flute is to snare
(C)   saxophone is to violin
(D)   cello is to harpsichord
(E)   piano is to xylophone

59.   Canyon is to river as:

(A)   swimming pool is to water
(B)   strait is to bay
(C)   plateau is to precipice
(D)   mountain is to island
(E)   tides are to moon

64

60.   Hangar is to airplane as:

(A)   truck is to truck stop
(B)   helicopter is to helipad
(C)   ambulance is to hospital
(D)   garage is to car
(E)   motorcycle is to bicycle

61.   Optometrist is to eyes as podiatrist is to:

(A)   skin
(B)   heart
(C)   hands
(D)   lungs
(E)   feet

62.   Anthology is to music as:

(A)   apple is to worm
(B)   menu is to restaurant
(C)   tile is to mosaic
(D)   album is to photographs
(E)   cookies is to jar

63:     Coastline is to continent as:

(A)   camel is to desert
(B)   margin is to paper
(C)   fjord is to inlet
(D)   strait is to land
(E)   peninsula is to ship

64.   Agitator is to incite as:

(A)   realtor is to buy
(B)   lawyer is to represent
(C)   mathematician is to prove
(D)   investor is to save
(E)   detractor is to depress

64. Astrology is to astronomy as:

(A)   biology is to physics
(B)   botany is to plants
(C)   alchemy is to chemistry
(D)   animals is to zoology
(E)   theology is to religion

65. Intermission is to play as:

(A)   anthem is to sport
(B)   credits is to movie
(C)   sleep is to night
(D)   half-time is to football
(E)   victuals is to meal

66. Tariff is to goods as:

(A)   tithe is to church
(B)   complimentary is to item
(C)   tip is to service
(D)   bonus is to salary
(E)   income is to work

67. Artery is to vein as:

(A)   emigration is to immigration
(B)   glass is to cup
(C)   orange is to tangerine
(D)   inch is to foot
(E)   open is to closed

68. Coda is to music as:

(A)   subtext is to movie
(B)   abstract is to concrete
(C)   dedication is to art
(D)   epilogue is to book
(E)   sequel is to ending

69. Elegy is do poem as:

(A) flabbergasted is to editorial
(B) comedy is to poem
(C) comedic is to video
(D) vibrant is to portrait
(E) dirge is to song

70. Claw is to cat as:

(A) talon is to eagle
(B) paw is to dog
(C) snout is to pig
(D) hand is to monkey
(E) trunk is to elephant

71. Pentagon is to perimeter as:

(A) square is to area
(B) trapezoid is to median
(C) triangle is to angle
(D) circle is to circumference
(E) cylinder is to volume

72. Crude is to tact as:

(A) flummox is to disorganized
(B) impromptu is to plan
(C) stupid is to brain
(D) outline is to plan
(E) yield is to restrain

73. Excerpt is to book as:

(A) volume is to set
(B) curtain is to drape
(C) beagle is to collie
(D) clip is to film
(E) grain is to rice

74. Masticate is to chew as:

(A) whiff is to digest
(B) exhale is to swallow
(C) imbibe is to drink
(D) barter is to donate
(E) purloin is to give

75. Arboreal is to tree as:

(A) ligneous is to wood
(B) extraterrestrial is to UFO
(C) aquatic is to water
(D) complex is to comprehend
(E) soft is to mushy

76. Blue is to red as:

(A) sad is to angry
(B) warning is to frightening
(C) cautious is to envious
(D) warm is to cold
(E) primary is to secondary

77. Eavesdrop is to listen as:

(A) color is to draw
(B) purloin is to take
(C) signal is to indicate
(D) snoop is to look
(E) splurge is to disclose

78. Labyrinth is to Byzantine as:

(A) quaint is to metropolitan
(B) alley is to lengthen
(C) austere is to Spartan
(D) Bible is to Corinthian
(E) lenient is to draconian

79.   Copper is to mine as:

(A)   silver is to alloy
(B)   strawberry is to jam
(C)   egg is to carton
(D)   fusion is to fission
(E)   limestone is to quarry

80.   Watermelon is to rind as:

(A)   skin is to pear
(B)   banana is to peel
(C)   leaf is to tree
(D)   seed is to grape
(E)   seed is to cherry

81.   Panegyric is to praise as:

(A)   oration is to ignore
(B)   libel is to denigrate
(C)   diatribe is to encourage
(D)   ballad is to celebrate
(E)   invective is to motivate

82.   Revolution is to sun as:

(A)   gyroscope is to string
(B)   evolution is to human
(C)   nocturnal is to night
(D)   periodic is to climate
(E)   rotation is to axis

83.   Love is to fetish as:

(A)   confuse is to perplex
(B)   amuse is to adore
(C)   rancor is to irk
(D)   weep is to cry
(E)   bother is to insidious

84.   Perspicacious is to imperceptive as:

(A)   joyous is to jolly
(B)   mawkish is to mushy
(C)   emotive is to stolid
(D)   pragmatic is to hardheaded
(E)   obnoxious is to dumb

85.   Mayor is to municipal as:

(A)   queen is to regal
(B)   yahoo is to provincial
(C)   president is to national
(D)   dictator is to tyrannical
(E)   governor is to general

86.   Game is to win as:

(A)   experiment is to results
(B)   smell to digest
(C)   taste is to eat
(D)   walk is to exercise
(E)   politician is to candidate

87.   Crescendo is to climax as:

(A)   refrain is to typical
(B)   repeat is to pattern
(C)   wane is to wax
(D)   score is to music
(E)   pause is to lull

88.   Mitosis is to bifurcation as:

(A)   rebuilding is to annexation
(B)   dying is to karma
(C)   success is to rumination
(D)   puberty is to metamorphosis
(E)   melding is to alloy

89.   Incarcerate is to imprison as:

(A)   chastise is to bestow
(B)   enumerate is to erase
(C)   eviscerate is to encourage
(D)   validate is to sanction
(E)   permit is to deny

90.   Soirée is to party as:

(A)   beauty is to pageant
(B)   prospectus is to book
(C)   sneak peek is to movie
(D)   matinee is to movie
(E)   supper is to meal

91.   Quiver is to arrows as:

(A)   balloon is to helium
(B)   wallet is to cash
(C)   tendon is to ligament
(D)   candle is to wick
(E)   aquarium is to goldfish

92.   Éclair is to custard as:

(A)   dress is to sequins
(B)   yearbook is to pictures
(C)   television is to commercials
(D)   table is to legs
(E)   pillow is to down

93.   Prognostication is to hindsight as:

(A)   hors d'oeuvre is to meal
(B)   overture is to encore
(C)   introduction is to intermission
(D)   serendipitous is to portentous
(E)   reflective is to concocted

94.   Approximate is to exact as:

(A)   law is to formula
(B)   rough is to calculated
(C)   trial is to conclusion
(D)   inference is to data
(E)   extrapolation is to evidence

95.   Illiterate is to words as:

(A)   illegitimate is to verified
(B)   innumerate is to numbers
(C)   improper is to manners
(D)   inept is to slyness
(E)   irregular is to constancy

96.   Chameleon is to camouflage as:

(A)   giraffe is to neck
(B)   quill is to porcupine
(C)   venom is to snake
(D)   skunk is to odor
(E)   horse is to hoof

97.   Couplet is to two as:

(A)   quatrain is to four
(B)   monocle is to glasses
(C)   unknown is to obvious
(D)   three is to triceratops
(E)   lie is to truth

98.   Lion is to pride as:

(A)   rabbit is to carrot
(B)   school is to fish
(C)   pig is to swine
(D)   litter is to cat
(E)   crow is to murder

99.   Bellhop is to baggage as:

(A)   cowboy is to lasso
(B)   waiter is to meal
(C)   sheriff is to badge
(D)   director is to play
(E)   operator is to telephone

100.   Pantomime is to words as:

(A)   puppeteer is to marionette
(B)   entertaining is to colorful
(C)   monochrome is to color
(D)   string is to knot
(E)   boat is to motion

101.   Ape is to mimic as:

(A)   ignore is to deny
(B)   belch is to sing
(C)   create is to upkeep
(D)   etch is to erase
(E)   assent is to nod

102.   Steam is to waft as:

(A)   water is to drink
(B)   elevator is to rise
(C)   rain is to fall
(D)   mountain is to height
(E)   rock is to sedentary

103.   Synopsis is to book as:

(A)   disquisition is to ideas
(B)   preview is to exhibit
(C)   abstract is to article
(D)   review is to restaurant
(E)   subtitle is to inform

104.   Milk is to sour as:

(A)   bread is to moldy
(B)   orange is to marmalade
(C)   tomato is to ripe
(D)   rust is to iron
(E)   steak is to charred

105.   Gravity is to force as:

(A)   kilogram is to weight
(B)   light is to refraction
(C)   molecule is to isotope
(D)   mass is to size
(E)   sound is to wave

106.   Phoenix is to rebirth as:

(A)   warlock is to poison
(B)   dwarf is to elf
(C)   grim reaper is to death
(D)   cradle is to baby
(E)   knight is to dragon

107.   Prime Meridian is to Earth as:

(A)   yin is to yang
(B)   left is to right
(C)   county is to state
(D)   winter is to summer
(E)   median is to highway

108.   Invitation is to party as:

(A)   termination is to business
(B)   obituary is to death
(C)   offer is to employment
(D)   envelope is to package
(E)   flag is to nation

109. Gamble is to money as:

(A)   trust is to friendship
(B)   adultery is to divorce
(C)   promulgate is to writing
(D)   skydiving is to life
(E)   magic is to illusion

110. Season is to cyclical as:

(A)   climate is to understandable
(B)   supporter is to loyal
(C)   day is to diurnal
(D)   weather is to predictable
(E)   year is to sequential

111. Unsettle is to destabilize as:

(A)   fascinate is to captivate
(B)   delight is to tickle
(C)   beleaguer is to question
(D)   possess is to own
(E)   harm is to annoy

112. Circle is to vertex as:

(A)   desert is to precipitation
(B)   word is to syllable
(C)   artifact is to museum
(D)   albino is to pigment
(E)   ocean is to fish

113. Strand is to hair as:

(A)   hornet is to nest
(B)   bifocals are to eyes
(C)   tooth is to comb
(D)   library is to book
(E)   wool is to sheep

114. Win is to landslide as:

(A)   tie is to draw
(B)   success is to achievement
(C)   black is to midnight
(D)   loss is to obliteration
(E)   delay is to hindrance

115. Policeman is to ticket as:

(A)   teacher is to attendance
(B)   rabbi is to funeral
(C)   cook is to meal
(D)   doctor is to prescription
(E)   clown is to balloon

116. Speed is to direction as:

(A)   velocity is to mileage
(B)   pollution is to chemicals
(C)   blackboard is to chalk
(D)   compass is to needle
(E)   ambiguity is to clarity

117. Novella is to tome as:

(A)   commentary is to blurb
(B)   canoe is to cruise ship
(C)   romance is to mystery
(D)   jingle is to song
(E)   store is to shop

118. Oily is to viscous as:

(A)   gooey is to slimy
(B)   silky is to dirty
(C)   melodramatic is to intense
(D)   ribald is to offensive
(E)   boorish is to refined

119. Metronome is to tempo as:

(A) keys are to car
(B) motor is to engine
(C) odometer is to speed
(D) clock is to time
(E) radio is to sound

120. Flight number is to route as:

(A) butter is to bread
(B) beaker is to liquid
(C) compassion is to kindness
(D) copyright is to publication
(E) barcode is to object

ANSWER KEY

SYNONYMS:

1.	A	41.	C	81.	A
2.	C	42.	E	82.	D
3.	E	43.	D	83.	C
4.	C	44.	B	84.	E
5.	D	45.	B	85.	B
6.	C	46.	C	86.	A
7.	B	47.	C	87.	C
8.	E	48.	B	88.	D
9.	C	49.	E	89.	B
10.	B	50.	E	90.	E
11.	C	51.	B	91.	A
12.	A	52.	B	92.	C
13.	B	53.	D	93.	C
14.	E	54.	B	94.	B
15.	A	55.	C	95.	A
16.	D	56.	B	96.	E
17.	B	57.	B	97.	D
18.	C	58.	C	98.	B
19.	A	59.	B	99.	A
20.	A	60.	E	100.	B
21.	C	61.	B	101.	A
22.	D	62.	A	102.	B
23.	A	63.	C	103.	C
24.	B	64.	E	104.	E
25.	C	65.	A	105.	B
26.	C	66.	B	106.	C
27.	A	67.	C	107.	E
28.	A	68.	C	108.	C
29.	E	69.	D	109.	B
30.	D	70.	E	110.	B
31.	B	71.	B	111.	C
32.	E	72.	D	112.	E
33.	C	73.	A	113.	C
34.	D	74.	C	114.	D
35.	B	75.	A	115.	B
36.	A	76.	B	116.	A
37.	A	77.	A	117.	C
38.	A	78.	C	118.	A
39.	C	79.	B	119.	A
40.	E	80.	C	120.	A

121.	C		167.	A		213.	D
122.	A		168.	D		214.	C
123.	A		169.	B		215.	A
124.	D		170.	B		216.	D
125.	B		171.	A		217.	A
126.	D		172.	E		218.	B
127.	A		173.	E		219.	E
128.	C		174.	B		220.	B
129.	E		175.	B		221.	E
130.	C		176.	E		222.	D
131.	B		177.	B		223.	B
132.	D		178.	E		224.	C
133.	C		179.	E		225.	E
134.	B		180.	C		226.	B
135.	B		181.	A		227.	D
136.	D		182.	B		228.	E
137.	E		183.	E		229.	A
138.	C		184.	B		230.	D
139.	B		185.	C		231.	D
140.	A		186.	D		232.	E
141.	E		187.	D		233.	C
142.	B		188.	E		234.	C
143.	A		189.	A		235.	A
144.	E		190.	B		236.	C
145.	D		191.	C		237.	B
146.	C		192.	A		238.	E
147.	D		193.	D		239.	B
148.	E		194.	B		240.	A
149.	D		195.	C		241.	C
150.	B		196.	E		242.	B
151.	C		197.	A		243.	A
152.	B		198.	D		244.	C
153.	B		199.	A		245.	D
154.	A		200.	C			
155.	D		201.	C			
156.	B		202.	E			
157.	C		203.	B			
158.	B		204.	C			
159.	C		205.	D			
160.	E		206.	A			
161.	D		207.	B			
162.	B		208.	C			
163.	E		209.	A			
164.	B		210.	B			
165.	A		211.	E			
166.	D		212.	B			

ANALOGY SOLUTIONS:

#	Ans	#	Ans	#	Ans
1.	C	39.	B	80.	B
2.	E	40.	B	81.	B
3.	D	41.	A	82.	E
4.	B	42.	E	83.	C
5.	C	43.	D	84.	C
6.	B	44.	C	85.	C
7.	E	45.	D	86.	A
8.	A	46.	A	87.	E
9.	D	47.	D	88.	D
10.	C	48.	C	89.	D
11.	B	49.	E	90.	E
12.	C	50.	A	91.	B
13.	E	51.	B	92.	E
14.	B	52.	A	93.	B
15.	D	53.	E	94.	B
16.	E	54.	E	95.	B
17.	D	55.	D	96.	D
18.	E	56.	A	97.	A
19.	D	57.	D	98.	E
20.	A	58.	B	99.	B
21.	B	59.	E	100.	C
22.	C	60.	D	101.	E
23.	C	61.	E	102.	C
24.	C	62.	D	103.	C
25.	B	63.	B	104.	A
26.	B	64.	C	105.	E
27.	D	65.	D	106.	C
28.	B	66.	A	107.	E
29.	D	67.	A	108.	C
30.	D	68.	D	109.	D
31.	C	69.	E	110.	E
32.	A	70.	A	111.	A
33.	E	71.	D	112.	D
34.	B	72.	B	113.	C
35.	C	73.	D	114.	D
36.	E	74.	C	115.	D
37.	C	75.	C	116.	E
38.	A	76.	A	117.	B
		77.	D	118.	E
		78.	C	119.	D
		79.	E	120.	E

HINTS FOR SOLVING ANALOGY QUESTIONS:

1. a coven is a group of witches
2. frozen and gelid both refer to the state of being extremely cold
3. Saturn is a specific example of a planet
4. parched and inundated are antonyms
5. something that is soporific makes one sleepy
6. the implement for ingesting soup is a spoon
7. something that is dubious causes doubt
8. a lack of sleep leads to insomnia
9. a drip is a small amount of water; a flood is a large amount of water
10. a Dalmatian is a type of dog
11. to polish is to burnish
12. an apostate is one who has little or no regard for sacrosanct things
13. an architect creates a product which often later requires the expertise of an electrician to complete
14. a story measures the height of something above the ground
15. a roster is a list of names
16. green is the color of emeralds
17. a pen is an implement that one holds in one's hands for writing
18. the intensity of sound is measured in decibels
19. something that is an accident is not deliberate
20. a comedy is a type or genre of film
21. to lampoon someone is to mock him or her
22. a circle imagined in three dimensions is a sphere
23. baseball is played on a diamond
24. a kangaroo is a type of marsupial
25. discordant is an adjective that refers to an unpleasant sound
26. a sigh is a noise one makes to indicate relief
27. a caboose comes at the end of a train
28. one cites something in order to understand and acknowledge a point
29. oil is made from olives
30. the goal of a politician is to obtain votes
31. to deny is to not acknowledge
32. to nibble is to eat just a little; to devour is to consume in great amounts
33. a chapter is a (numbered) part of a book
34. a toucan is an animal (bird) that lives in the rainforest
35. an inherent quality of a magnet is the ability to attract things
36. to vanquish is to defeat thoroughly; to suppress is less extreme and is to stop or contain
37. to flourish is the opposite of to decay
38. an apprentice is someone who is new at something whereas an expert is skilled
39. a peanut is a type of legume
40. a naysayer is someone inclined to deny something

41. an itinerary is a schedule for a trip
42. scissors are a tool used to cut one's hair
43. someone who is extroverted is outgoing
44. something or someone transparent is not opaque
45. to mitigate is to assuage
46. to emancipate is to free
47. certain clouds contain or produce rain
48. to raze is to destroy
49. one launches a rocket to set it in motion in the air
50. an alibi is someone or something that provides a pretext that explains someone's whereabouts and thus innocence in a crime
51. emaciated is extremely thin
52. a tadpole turns into a frog as it matures
53. a lever swings about a fulcrum
54. a thermometer measures temperature
55. something that is baroque is ornate
56. a famine indicates a widespread lack of food
57. a mountain juts out of the land; a crater is a sink in the land
58. a clarinet is a woodwind instrument and a tympani is a type of drum or percussion instrument
59. a canyon is caused by a river
60. airplanes are housed and serviced in a hangar
61. an optometrist is an eye doctor
62. an anthology contains a collection of music
63. a coastline typically is at the edge of a continent
64. astrology is a non-quantitative, non-rigorous study of the stars (for horoscopes) whereas astronomy is scientific and rigorous
65. an intermission is a pause, usually around midway through a play
66. a tariff is a tax to be paid for goods
67. an artery carries blood outward from the heart, a vein carries blood inward to the heart
68. a coda comes at the end of a piece of music
69. an elegy is a mournful poem
70. a claw on the paws of a cat is what a cat uses to attack, scratch, or defend itself
71. the perimeter is the boundary of a polygonal region (and a pentagon is a polygon with five sides)
72. to be crude is to lack tact
73. an excerpt is piece of a book
74. to masticate is to chew
75. a creature that is arboreal lives in a tree
76. someone who is blue is sad; someone who is red is angry
77. to eavesdrop is to listen secretly with the hope that nobody will notice
78. a labyrinth would be described as Byzantine
79. copper is extracted from a mine
80. the rind is the inedible outside part of a watermelon

81. a panegyric consists of words that praise someone
82. a planet revolves about the sun
83. a fetish is a shallow form of liking whereas love is a much more intense liking
84. one who is perspicacious is not imperceptive
85. a mayor governs things at a municipal level
86. the goal of a game is to win
87. a crescendo is indicative of a climax
88. bifurcation occurs during mitosis
89. to incarcerate is to imprison
90. a soirée is an evening party
91. a quiver is a pouch for holding arrows
92. an éclair is filled with custard
93. prognostication involves seeing something in advance whereas hindsight is reflecting upon something after it has happened
94. something that's approximate is an estimation, but is not exact
95. to be illiterate is to be unable to read or to lack a basic knowledge of words
96. a chameleon uses camouflage to protect itself
97. a couplet is two lines of verse
98. a group of lions is called a pride
99. a bellhop is someone who carries your luggage for you
100. a pantomime does not use words
101. to mimic is to ape
102. steam wafts through the air
103. a synopsis is a brief summary of a book
104. when milk goes stale it becomes sour
105. gravity is a type of force
106. a phoenix is a mythical symbol of rebirth
107. the Prime Meridian divides the Earth into two parts
108. an invitation is a written statement welcoming one to a party
109. gambling is an activity that can put one's money at risk
110. seasons occur every year in a cycle
111. to destabilize is to very heavily unsettle
112. a circle does not contain a vertex
113. a strand is a piece of hair
114. a landslide is to win by a huge margin
115. a policeman writes a ticket to someone for them to manage
116. speed is a quantity that lacks direction (it is expressed in magnitude only)
117. a novella is a small version of a book; a tome is a giant book
118. something oily is not viscous
119. a metronome helps one measure or keep tempo
120. a flight number allows one to track a flight route

ABOUT THE AUTHOR

Justin Grosslight is an academic entrepreneur interested in examining relationships between science and business. He is especially intrigued by how networks operate (quantitatively and qualitatively), both from historical and from contemporary perspectives. He holds degrees in history and mathematics from Stanford, a history of science degree from Harvard, and has published in all three fields. He is passionate about business, entertainment, academia, and writing, and enjoys helping talented youth thrive in their intellectual pursuits.

Justin has had years of experience in training students for their SAT®, SSAT®, ACT®, GMAT®, GRE®, AP® Calculus, IB® mathematics, SAT® physics subject test, and SAT® mathematics subject tests. He is a national merit scholar who received a perfect 800 on his SAT® math exam, perfect 800 on his SAT® math level 2 subject test, perfect 170 on his GRE® math exam, perfect 5 on his AP® Calculus BC exam (as a sophomore), perfect 5 on his AP® US History Exam, perfect 6 on his GMAT® writing exam, a perfect 8 on his GMAT® integrated reasoning exam, and near perfect scores on all of his other exams. He has published widely in both the humanities and in mathematics.

Several of Justin's students have received perfect scores on sections of their SAT® and ACT® exams, on their SAT® math subject test, and on their SAT® physics subject test. They have gained admission into prestigious universities such as Stanford University, NYU, UCLA, The University of Pennsylvania, and Oberlin College.

ABOUT MANDA EDUCATION

Manda Education is a test preparation program that believes in helping students whet their educational skills through personalized training. Realizing that different students have different needs, Manda Education believes that the best way to train students was to mentor them in both a personalized and intensive framework. Our aims are threefold:

(1)   To help students achieve test scores that will gain them admittance to universities of their choice
(2)   To develop writing, communication, quantitative, and analytical skills that will help students flourish in a global context
(3)   To instill values of character and responsibility in students that will help students succeed in their personal and professional endeavors

We also believe that many students and professionals can benefit from our books, so we have released them for sale to the public.

Made in the USA
Columbia, SC
28 October 2017